Mel Bay Presents... The Guitar Master

BARRY GALBRAITH
GUITAR SOLOS

THIRTEEN STANDARDS
compiled by Jim Lichens
Volume 2

MW01153346

CD contents

1	Tuning Note [:28]	8	A Certain Smile [1:15]
2	I've Grown Accustomed to Her Face [1:33]	9	Our Love is Here to Stay [1:36]
3	Satin Doll [1:13]	10	Here's that Rainy Day [2:04]
4	Last Night When We Were Young [2:08]	11	How About You? [1:35]
5	Imagination [1:40]	12	I Cover the Waterfront [2:12]
6	Somebody Loves Me [:55]	13	Love Walked In [2:07]
7	Come Rain or Come Shine [1:04]	14	Yesterdays [1:59]

1 2 3 4 5 6 7 8 9 0

Visit us on the Web at www.melbay.com — E-mail us at email@melbay.com

Contents

Introduction

For years, only a handful of guitar players have known about Barry Galbraith's arrangements. Now, thanks to the efforts of many people, we are all able to see, hear, study, and play these wonderful guitar solos.

I would, first of all, like to thank my mother. She had the foresight (in 1950) to enroll me with a guitar teacher that taught me to read and write music. Thanks, Mom! My wife, Jacquie, has never ceased encouraging me to do this project. She also helped design the cover of the first volume. Don Galbraith, Barry's son, has helped us from the beginning. Allen Johnson and Len Williams spent many hours smoothing out the final manuscripts. John Purse did the final engravings, "fixed" what we missed, and performed the arrangements on the companion CD. John always amazes us with his many talents. Jim Hall was very kind to review the first volume in Just Jazz Guitar magazine. Finally, we are grateful for Bill Bay and the folks at Mel Bay Publications for having the vision and ability to make these arrangements available.

We hope that, through these arrangements, you will experience the joy of Barry Galbraith's incredible talent.

Keep on pickin',

Jim Lichens

SoloFlt1@comcast.net

I've Grown Accustomed to Her Face

Arr. by BARRY GALBRAITH

Words by ALAN JAY LERNER
Music by FREDERICK LOEWE

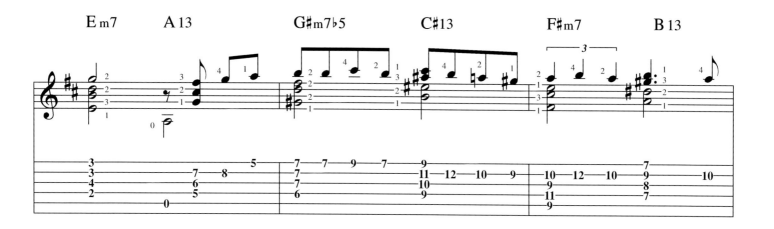

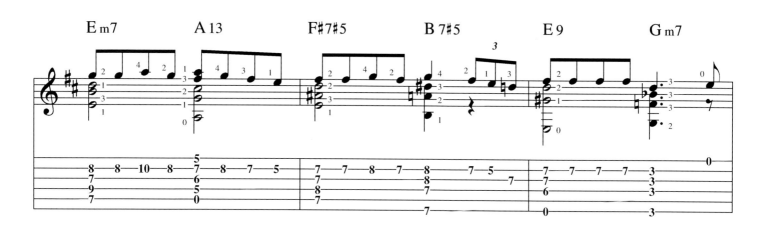

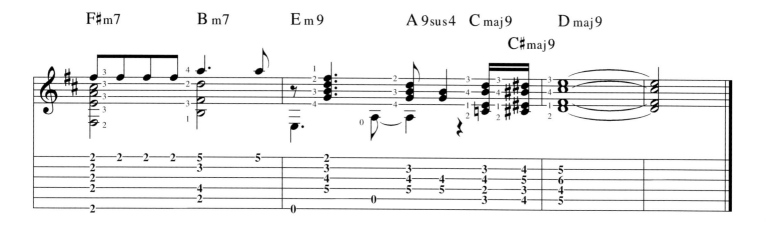

Satin Doll

Arr. by BARRY GALBRAITH

By JOHNNY MERCER,
DUKE ELLINGTON and
BILLY STRAYHORN

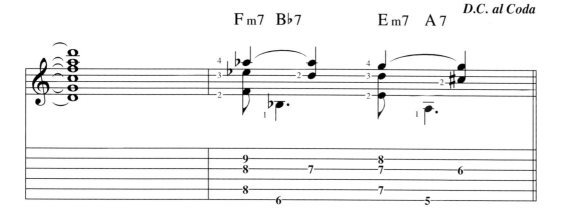

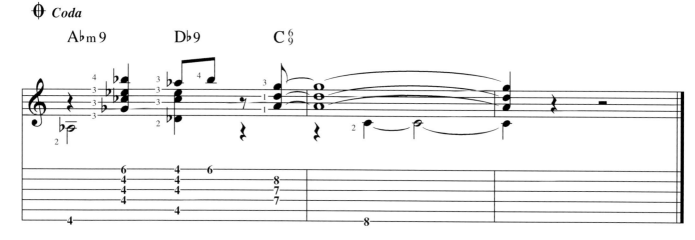

Last Night When We Were Young

Arr. by BARRY GALBRAITH

Words by E. Y. HARBURG
Music by HAROLD ARLEN

Imagination

Arr. by BARRY GALBRAITH

Words by JOHNNY BURKE
Music by JIMMY VAN HEUSEN

D.S. al Coda

* Barry left the last two measures to our imagination!

11

Somebody Loves Me

Arr. by BARRY GALBRAITH

Words by B. G. DeSYLVA and
BALLARD MACDONALD
Music by GEORGE GERSHWIN

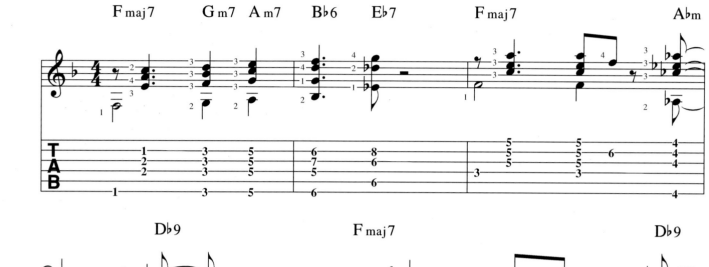

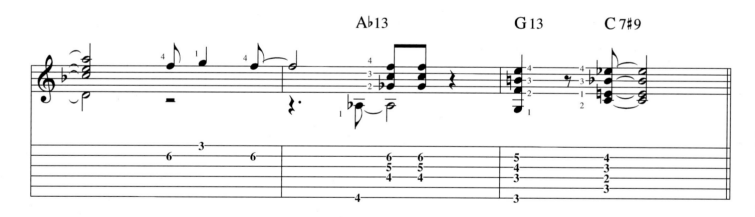

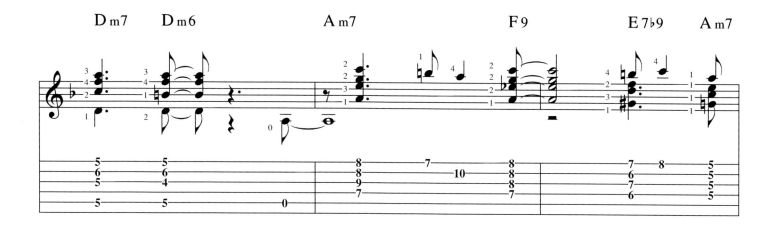

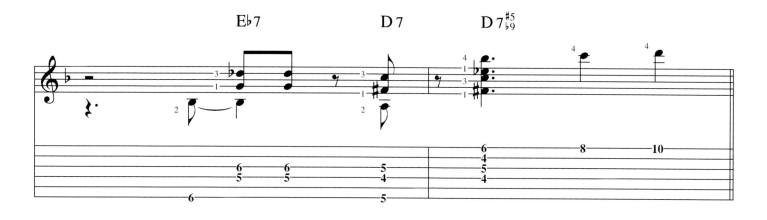

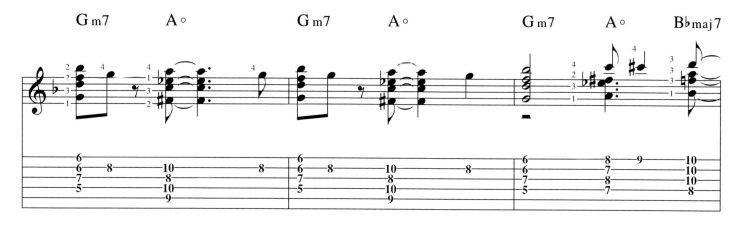

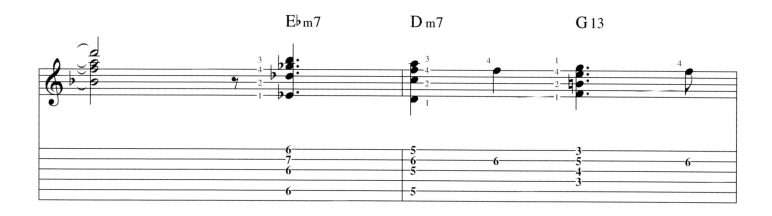

This page has been left blank to avoid awkward page turns.

Come Rain or Come Shine

Arr. by BARRY GALBRAITH

Music by HAROLD ARLEN
Words by JOHNNY MERCER

A Certain Smile

Arr. by BARRY GALBRAITH

By SAMMY FAIN and
PAUL FRANCIS WEBSTER

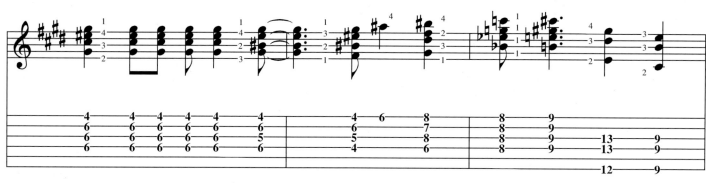

18

Our Love is Here to Stay

Arr. by BARRY GALBRAITH

By GEORGE and
IRA GERSHWIN

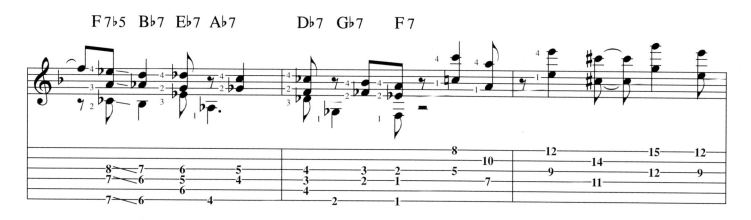

Here's that Rainy Day

Arr. by BARRY GALBRAITH

Words by JOHNNY BURKE
Music by JIMMY VAN HEUSEN

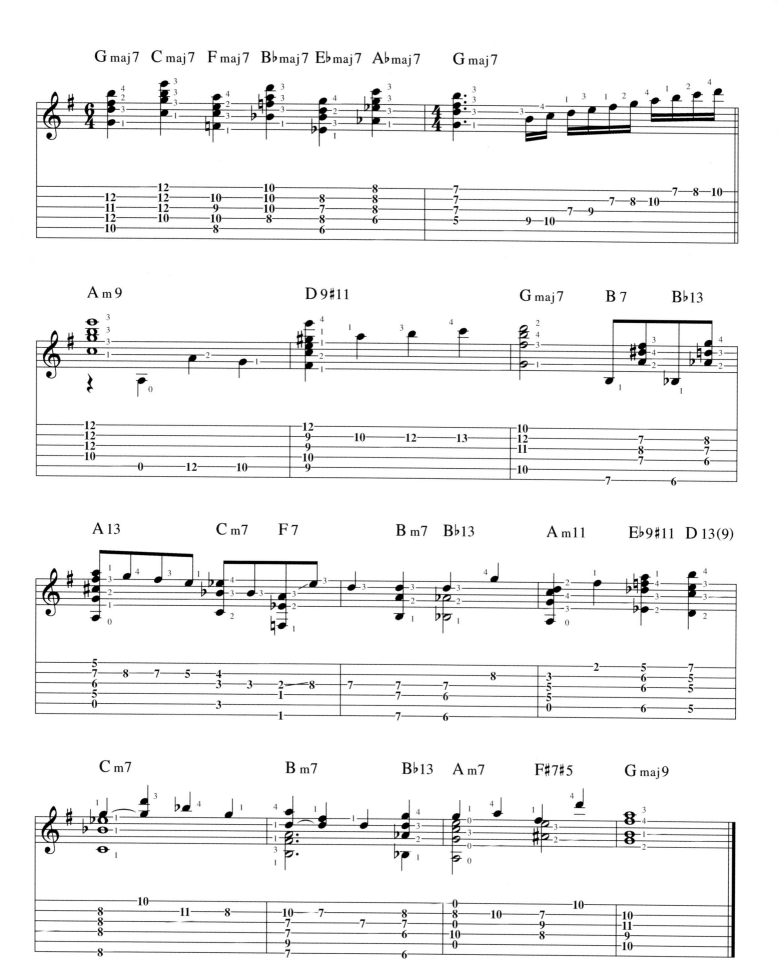

How About You?

Arr. by BARRY GALBRAITH

Words by BURTON LANE
Music by RALPH FREED

*This page has been
left blank to avoid
awkward page turns.*

I Cover the Waterfront

Arr. by BARRY GALBRAITH

Words by EDWARD HEYMAN
Music by JOHN GREEN

30

Love Walked in

Arr. by BARRY GALBRAITH

By GEORGE and IRA GERSHWIN

33

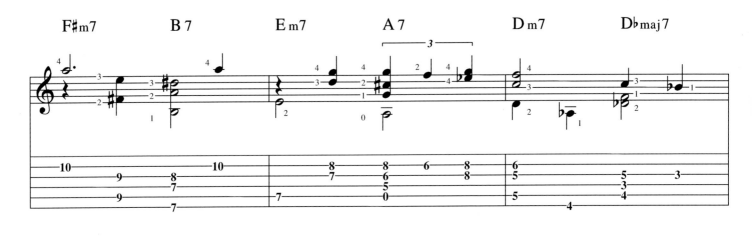

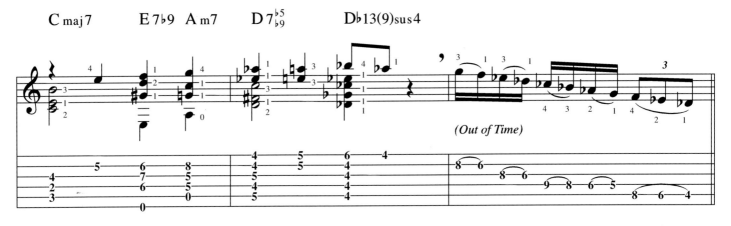

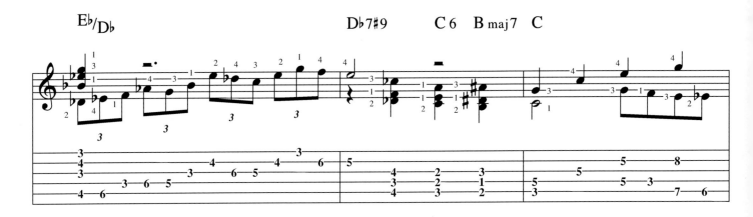

Yesterdays

Arr. by BARRY GALBRAITH

Words by OTTO HARBACH
Music by JEROME KERN

EXCELLENCE IN MUSIC
MEL BAY®
Since 1947